THIRTY-SIX
PSALMS

T0382494

THIRTY-SIX PSALMS

AN ENGLISH VERSION

BY

FRANK KENDON

CAMBRIDGE

AT THE UNIVERSITY PRESS

1963

CAMBRIDGE UNIVERSITY PRESS
Cambridge, New York, Melbourne, Madrid, Cape Town, Singapore, São Paulo, Delhi

Cambridge University Press
The Edinburgh Building, Cambridge CB2 8RU, UK

Published in the United States of America by Cambridge University Press, New York

www.cambridge.org
Information on this title: www.cambridge.org/9780521103251

© Cambridge University Press 1963

First published 1963
This digitally printed version 2009

A catalogue record for this publication is available from the British Library

ISBN 978-0-521-07153-6 hardback
ISBN 978-0-521-10325-1 paperback

A NOTE ON THE TRANSLATION

When plans were being made for the New English Bible it was natural that the work of putting the Psalms into appropriate English should be entrusted to a poet. Frank Kendon was invited to take the basic draft provided by the panel of translators, and to rework it so that the qualities of the Hebrew original should in some measure be recreated. His second draft was to go for final revision to the Literary Committee of the translators, which was responsible for working on the translators' drafts of the other parts of the Bible, and concerned itself principally with style.

His work on the Psalms was Kendon's main concern in the last years of his life, until failing health prevented further work. He thought hard about the task as he went on with it, and became committed to a point of view, which he expressed in two notes. The first is formal, to the Literary Panel as a whole:

'One general remark I feel called upon to make. One passionate opposition we are to expect to our version will be from readers who are familiar with the very words and cadences of the Authorized Version. This offence cannot be entirely avoided. In many passages the Authorized

Version has now said what cannot be better said aesthetically; we cannot deny this. But I think we can prevent it from being an angry (and, of course, partly irrelevant) effect in the minds of such readers. Psalm 19 is a case in point. If our version is continually almost recalling the familiar Authorized Version then the places where, because of subsequent more exact Hebrew knowledge, our version must be different will be the places where such readers' aesthetic feelings will be shocked. If a psalm starts off with an oasis like: "The heavens declare the glory of God, and the firmament showeth his handiwork" and then goes on to differ more or less widely, a wrong kind of attention will be directed, in these conservative minds, to its points of variation; whereas, I would maintain, if through new rhythms and acceptable alternative expressions Psalm 19 can dawn upon them (to put it unsubtly) as a poem new to them, they will not immediately be provoked to automatic opposition. I have become aware of this particularly in dealing with the Psalms, and I have sometimes for this clear reason tried for a freshness of rhythm, of sentence form, and of alternative words.

'I suppose a psalm, fundamentally, is intrinsic, and does not dwell in the words that express it, but in the feeling that troubles the mind of David and the mind of his reader. It is conceivable that a succession of single words, each judged "accurate", may in its string of words (how, one does not know) lose its truth of feeling. In our work I think (giving a comparison with the microscope) the use of a high power of magnification of a small field has its dangers; and I advocate also, and more importantly, a low power and a large field, as when we rendered Wisdom's "I am thy bondservant and the son of thy handmaiden" as "I am born and bred thy servant". We are building (under God) a machine to our hands and minds far more complicated, if I may say so, than the electronic computer; and while Hebrew and Greek exactitude must occupy important parts of it we have to make provision also for piety, literary beauty, and inspiration or imagination.'

The second is from a private note sent to Dr C. H. Dodd, the Director of the whole translation, with his draft of the first seventeen psalms:

'I am satisfied with them, and satisfied in my heart that I can't do them better, though I think they get better as I get more practised. I want to say that I have been *rigidly* conscientious in sticking to the imagery and the meaning of the Panel's drafts; that there is not a word or a phrase but has had drawn-out consideration from me, and I believe them to be faithful, nothing added to them, nothing of the Draft left out. I have too, I believe, been faithful to the general direction of the Joint Committee, always remembering that the first aim is to make the language undisturbing and transparent and cogent for the audiences of the present day. In fact I have myself acted as a panel, quite unremittingly.'

All the Psalms were in some measure revised by the Literary Panel, but if Kendon's first draft is compared with the final version the Panel's changes are seen to be slight; and they never obscured Kendon's personal style. 'The Panel was very conscious', Dr Dodd writes, 'that it was dealing with the work of a poet, which ought to be treated with the respect due to such work, and not tampered with except where it was felt to be quite necessary. And down to 34, I think, Kendon was present and assented to the revision.' This version is therefore printed here as his agreed final draft.

Kendon's illness and death meant that the translators were left with an uncompleted work of marked individuality. It was decided to start afresh rather than to try to provide a pastiche of his style for the remaining Psalms. But these Psalms are now published because of their own merit, and as a memorial, by the Syndics of the Press, to whom he was Assistant Secretary, and by his colleagues there, who remember him with affection and respect as a good and gifted man, of whom it could truly be said

> *Who may ascend the mountain of the Lord?*
> *Who may stand upright in his holy place?*
> *He whose hands are clean and his heart pure,*
> *Who has not set his heart on worthless things.*

THE PSALMS

— 1 —

CALL that man happy who is never misled by evil advice,
  Who neither loiters where sinners pass
Nor chooses to sit down amongst the arrogant,
  But delights in the law of the Lord
And in that law meditates day and night.
  He is like a tree growing where rills of water run,
Fruitful in season and unwithered of leaf;
  In all that he does he prospers.

Bad men are not like this:
  They are chaff tossed aside by the wind;
In sessions of judgment, therefore, of no effect at all;
  Neither are sinners in a roomful of good men.
For the Lord remembers the ways of the law-abiding;
  The courses of wicked men end in ruin.

WHY this angry tumult among the nations?
   Why do the foreigners mutter among themselves vain mischief?
Earth's kings take their stand, and rulers plot together
   Against the Lord and his anointed king,
'Let us break their ropes' they say, 'and throw off all these coils.'

Enthroned in high heaven, the Lord laughs at them;
   He mocks them, and with angry words confronts them in his fury,
But I, on Zion's holy mountain, I have been made his king;
   I will declare you the Lord's own decree:
'You are my son' he said, 'this very day have I engendered you;
   Only ask me, and I will give you the nations for an inheritance,
And as far as earth stretches, your possessions shall extend;
   You shall break them with a bar of iron,
                 and smash them down like a clay pot.'
Look to it, therefore, O rulers of earth; O kings, be wary;
   See that you worship the Lord reverently;
Tremble before him and kiss his feet,
   Lest he grow angry, and you perish in your course,
For quick is the blaze of his anger.

Happy are all who find their refuge in him!

O LORD, my enemies come crowding upon me,
   They rise against me in swarms, saying of me one to another:
'Small help will he find in his God!'
   Whereas, O Lord, thou art indeed a shield to cover me;
Thou art my boast, thou by whom my head is held high.
   Loudly I cry to the Lord,
And he from his holy mountain answers me.
   I went to rest, I fell asleep, I woke: because the Lord bears me up.
I will not be afraid, though multitudes on every side beset me.
   Rise up, O Lord, O my God, rise up, and preserve me!

And surely thou hast; my enemies have felt thy blows
                              on their cheeks;
   Thou hast broken the teeth of the wicked ones.
The victory is the Lord's:
   Thy blessing rests upon thine own people!

ANSWER when I call, O God, defender of my right.
  Thou didst free me when I was hard pressed;
Be gracious to me and hear my prayer.
  O ye sons of men, O stubborn-hearted,
How long will you love what is vain and seek after falsity?
  Know this, that the Lord has shown me his constant love;
He hears me when I call.
  Be disquieted, but do not sin;
Have it out with your own heart in bed, and be silent;
  See that you make the sacrifice rightly expected of you,
And put your trust in the Lord.
  Many there are to say: 'If only someone
                                   would show us any good;
The light of thy presence, O Lord, has passed away from us.'
  Thou makest me more joyful of heart than men are when
                                   their corn and wine abound;
Now I will lie down at peace, and fall asleep,
  For thou alone, Lord, makest me live unafraid.

═ 5 ═

ATTEND, O Lord, to my spoken words,
                          and to the thoughts within me,
  And to my cry for help,
For to thee, my king and my God, to thee I bring my prayers.
  Early wilt thou hear my voice,
Early will I set out my sacrifice before thee,
  And early watch for thee.
Thou art not a god who delights in wickedness,
  Evil can be no guest of thine,
Boasters must fail before thy searching eyes,
  All mischief makers are hateful to thee,
Liars thou wilt destroy;
  The Lord detests all treacherous and bloodthirsty men.
But I, through thy great and faithful love,
                          may come into thy house,
  Towards thy holy temple I may stoop in reverence for thee.
Despite my slanderers, lead me, Lord, in thy justice;
  Keep me in thy straight path;
Nothing trustworthy ever passes their lips,
  They bluster within themselves,
And their throat is an open grave,
  And their tongue devoted to flattery.

Show up their crimes, O God;
   Let them fall, and by their own devices,
Fling them off because of their many rebellions,
                        and because they defy thee,
   But let all who find refuge with thee be joyful,
Breaking into shouts of joy again and again, and for ever.
   Give these thy care, that loving thy name,
                     they may exult in thee,
For thou wilt bless the righteous, O Lord,
   And wilt surround him, as with a shield, with thy favour.

6

O LORD, not in anger condemn me, not out of fury punish me,
  But be merciful to me, for I am weak and failing.
Heal me; my whole soul quivers, and my bones shake with terror.
  And thou, O Lord—how long?
Come back; set my soul free again,
  Even for the sake of thine own faithful heart save me, O Lord!
For death does not so remember thee;
  Who praises thee in that dark place?
I am worn out with my own groans;
  When, night after night, my pillow is soaked,
                                    and my bed dank with tears,
Grief dims my eyes,
  Too soon my sight grows old through my countless enemies.

Leave me and go, you trouble-makers, leave me,
  For the Lord has heard the sound of my weeping,
He has heard my pleading, and will accept my prayers.
  All my enemies shall quake with shame and terror;
If they come back at me, they shall suddenly be brought to shame.

O LORD, my God, in thee I hide from trouble,
  Save me from all my pursuers and set me free,
Lest as a lion they tear my throat and maul me
  With no one at hand to drag me clear.

O Lord my God, if I have done this,
  If indeed I am guilty of any wrong deed,
Or ever served badly one who meant me well,
  Or without reason let an enemy escape,
Then let my enemy chase and catch me,
  Trample my life, and lay my honour in the dust!

O Lord, in thy anger rise up,
  Rear thyself in fury against my foe,
Awake, O God, ordainer of judgment,
  Let the court of heaven assemble and gather round thee,
Take thy seat above them, enthroned on high,
  O Lord who judgest the nations.

Give me thy verdict, O Lord, according to my right
                                          and my innocence,
  And now bring ills that the wicked have done to an end.

But confirm thou the righteous:
   He who examines the heart and the inwardness,
                                          he is a just God.
My shield is this One Above All, is indeed God himself,
   The saviour of men of integrity.
God is the judge of the innocent, and a God roused
                                    every day to anger.

Once more the enemy sharpens his sword,
   Once more strings his bow, making it ready for shooting,
He sets all his deadly weapons in trim, tipping his arrows with fire.
   Watch him; he breeds mischief, he grows big with havoc,
                               and his brood is lies.
Has he not dug a hole in the ground, and dug it deep?
   But he it is who will fall into his own pit;
His mischief will come back upon him,
   His violence will but come raining down on his own head.

I will give due praise to the Lord for his justice.
   I will sing psalms to his name, the Lord Most High.

O LORD, our lord, how glorious thy name is,
                              the whole earth through;
    Whose majesty is extolled above the heavens themselves!
Even out of the mouths of babes newborn and nurslings
    Thou hast rebuked the mighty, because they are thy foes,
Making an end of enmity and revenge.
    As I look at the skies, the work of thy fingers,
At the moon and the stars, set where they are by thee,
    What is man, that thou shouldst think about him?
What is a son of man, to be cared for by thee?
    Yet hast thou made him little less than divine,
Crowning him with glory and honour,
    And giving him dominion over all that thy hands have made.
Everything lies under his feet by thy gift:
    Sheep and cattle, the wild beasts themselves,
Birds of the skies, fishes of the sea,
    And whatever makes way along ocean paths.
O Lord, our lord, how glorious, the wide earth through, thy name is!

9

WITH my whole heart I come to praise thee, Lord,
    And to tell the tale of all thy marvellous doings;
I shall be full of joy, and exult in thee,
    Singing hymns to thy name, O thou highest of all.
As soon as my enemies turn back they shall fall headlong,
    And perish from thy sight.

For thou hast upheld the justness of my cause;
    Thou art enthroned; thou art the unswerving judge;
Thou hast admonished the heathen; thou hast destroyed the wicked,
    Obliterating their name for evermore.

Enemies come to their end; their memory is dead and gone,
    Cities razed to the ground by thee are ruins for evermore.
But the Lord sits enthroned for ever;
    He has established his throne for judgment;
He and no other will judge the world in righteousness,
    And the sentence he gives to the peoples will be just and fair.
Thus may the Lord be a tower of strength for the oppressed—
    A tower of strength in time of need—
And those who cherish thy name, O Lord, may rely upon thee,
    Because thou dost not forsake those who look for thee.

11

Sing to the Lord who dwells in Zion:
   Among the nations tell of all he has done;
He who avenges blood has kept their longings in mind,
   He has not forgotten the cry of the poor.

Have pity on me, O Lord, look on my misery,
   Thou who dost raise and lift me up from the doors of death,
That I may tell the sum of thy praise;
   In the gates of the daughter of Zion I shall be glad indeed,
Being saved by thee.

The heathen flounder in a pit of their own digging;
   In the very net they had hidden their foot is snared.
The Lord has made himself known! He has carried
                                        out his sentence;
   The wicked are caught in the trap of their own misdeeds;
They shall turn back into darkness, all nations unmindful of God.

For the needy shall not always be forgotten,
   Nor shall the last hope of the poor be quenched.
Rise up, O Lord! Let not mere man brazen it out;
   Let the heathen be sentenced in thy presence.
Bring the truth home to them, O Lord!
   Let the nations learn that they are themselves but men.

WHY stand so far off, O Lord?
   Why hide thyself away in times of trouble?
Fiercely in their arrogance the wicked harry the poor:
   Let them be caught in snares of their own contriving!
For the wicked man boasts of his selfish heart;
   Greedy for gain, he curses the Lord, disdains him,
And, proudly, cares not to search for him;
   He leaves God out of account in every plan he makes.

Fixed for ever in his manner of life,
   Thy pronouncements passing by him unnoticed,
He scoffs at all his foes;
   Saying to himself, 'I shall never be shaken!'
He follows evil with untiring feet.

His mouth is full of slander and violent words;
   Mischief and strife lurk under his tongue;
He hides in ambush among the tents;
   In dark corners he murders his innocent victims,
His furtive eyes watch out for the unfortunate;
   Like a lion in his lair, so he in his hiding-place,
Lurking there, falls upon him who is poor;

Seizing the poor man, dragging him off in his net,

 crushed and cast down.

So fall the unhappy before his ruthless might;
 'God has forgotten,' his heart says,
'He has hidden his face, and will never notice.'

Rise up, O Lord! O God, lift up thy hand;
 Do not forget the poor.
Why has the wicked man rejected God
 And said in his heart, 'Thou dost not care'?
Indeed, thou hast seen his mischief and spite;
 Thou takest the matter into thine own hand.
He that is hapless places himself in thy charge;
 And who helps the fatherless but thou?
Break thou the arm of sin and wickedness,
 Hunt out all wickedness till there is no more of it.

The Lord is king everlasting,
 His land is rid of the heathen within.
O Lord, thou hast heard the lament of humble people
 And leaned thine ear to their hearts' desire,
To do justice to the fatherless and the oppressed,
 That men may no longer be driven in terror out of their land.

I HAVE found refuge in the Lord;
  How should you tell me, then,
To fly off to the mountain like a bird?
  See how, even now, the wicked are bending their bow,
And fitting arrow to cord,
  So as to shoot in secret at the upright-hearted.
If the foundations be broken down
  What can a just man do?

The Lord is in his holy temple—
  The Lord, whose throne is the sky.
His eyes are watching, and his eyelids questioning
                              the race of men,
  The Lord questions just and wicked alike;
And if a man have a mind to violence
  Him the Lord hates from his soul:
He shall shower down red-hot ashes on the wicked,
  Brimstone and a searing wind shall be in
                              the cup for them;
For the Lord is just, and loves deeds that are just;
  His face is turned toward him that is upright.

HELP, Lord, for now all loyalty is wanting,
   Good faith between man and man is at an end,
They lie to each other,
   In their talk, lips flatter and hearts cheat.

May the Lord cut away all such flattering lips
   And bragging tongues!
They who boasted, 'By our talk we gain importance.
   If our tongue serves us, who is our master then?'

Because of the robbery of the indigent,
   Because of the weeping of the needy,
'Now, now will I bestir myself', the Lord says;
   'I will ensure to him that safety which he yearns for.'

The words of the Lord are pure,
   As silver refined in a crucible,
As gold seven times purified.
   Save us, O Lord, save us,
Guard us from this corrupt and evil generation.
   The wicked go about openly on every hand,
While baseness is enthroned among mankind.

HOW long, O Lord, wilt thou entirely forget me?
  How long hide thy face?
How long must I harbour anguish in my being,
  Grief in my heart, day and night?
How long will my enemy be raised above me?

Look, now, O Lord my God, and answer me!
  Give these eyes light lest I sleep in death;
Lest my enemy claim, 'I have mastered him!'
  Or my foes be glad about my discomfiture.

But I have trusted to thy constancy;
  So let my heart rejoice in thy deliverance.
Let me sing to the Lord for all his bounty to me.

14

THE FOOL in his heart says, 'There is no God!'
  Corrupt are all their goings-on, and loathsome;
There is none that does good.

Out of the sky the Lord looked down among the sons of men
  To discover, if he could, anyone of understanding,
Anyone who sought after God:
  Everyone turns away; one and all are rotten at heart;
There is none that does good—no, not one.

And do they not care, these trouble-makers,
  Devouring my people as they would consume so much bread,
But never calling to the Lord?
  At that point they are seized with terror;
But God is amongst worthy men.
  You may put the poor man's counsels to shame:
But he finds a hiding-place in the Lord.

Oh that Israel's deliverance might come from Zion!
  When the Lord repairs the fortunes of his people
Let Jacob rejoice, let Israel be glad!

— 15 —

WHO, Lord, may be a guest in thy tent?
  Who may make his home in thy sacred mountain?
He whose life is blameless, he who does what is right
  And speaks from the heart what is true;
Whose tongue furthers no slander,
  Who treats no friend badly
Nor points the finger of reproach at his neighbour;
  Who respects no base fellow,
And honours the men who fear God;
  Who swears even to his own hurt
And keeps to his oath;
  Who does not lend money for gain,
And will not be bribed against innocence—
  The man who follows these courses shall never be shaken.

3-2

I HAVE found refuge in thee; O God therefore take care of me;
  I have said to the Lord, 'Thou art my happiness, Lord',
All the holy gods on earth are worthless;
  All who take delight in them are accurst.
They add to their troubles; they embitter their lot:
  I will not pour out drink-offerings of blood to them
Nor take the names of such gods on my lips.
  O Lord, thou portion due to me, the cup I drink from,
Thou dost add to the lot that falls to me;
  Truly my life now lies in pleasant places,
And I am delighted by what has come to me.
  The Lord has given me good counsel, and I will bless him;
At night the voice of my inmost being instructs me;
  I have set the Lord continually before me;
With him beside me I cannot be shaken;
  And so I am glad at heart, and my spirit exults,
And my body goes on living without a care.
  For thou dost not leave me to the place of darkness;
Thou wilt not suffer thy faithful one to see the abyss;
  Thou wilt show me the path of life;
Fullness of joy is in thy presence;
  In thy right hand are pleasures for ever and ever.

HEAR and heed, O Lord, my just appeal,
    Know that I cry to thee, listen to this my prayer;
No false word ever crosses my lips.
    Let my acquittal come from thy very presence.
See what is just.
    Thou hast examined my heart;
Thou hast come to me in the night;
    Thou hast put me to the proof and found no
                                    ill-purpose within.
My mouth shall not seem to forgive the doings of men.
    I have paid close heed to the word of thy lips.
My footsteps are firm in the path thou dost appoint,
    My feet have not slipped in thy ways.
I have called thee, O God, because thou dost answer me;
    Turn an ear my way; listen to what I ask;
Show me the wonder of thy enduring love,
    Thou saviour of them who seek safety in thee—
Safety from all who are rebels against thy right hand.
    As the apple of the eye, guard me,
In shelter of thy wings hide me away
    From the wicked who would do me violent harm,
The greedy foes who hem me round.

They have stifled their breath of pity;
Proudly their mouths speak,
   They rush straight at me, they surround me,
They watch for my downfall,
   Like a lion eager to maul its victim,
A young lion lurking in secret places!

O Lord, stand up; confront him; bring him to his knees;
   Save my life from the wicked,
With thy sword, with thy hand, O Lord, save me from such men,
   Men whose heritage in life is of this passing world,
Whose belly thou dost load with thy treasure,
   Who have numbers of children,
And bequeath all their surplus to them.

As for me, in righteousness I shall behold thy face;
   When I awake to my vision of thee I shall be satisfied.

—⟹ 18 ⟸—

I LOVE thee, O Lord, thou art my strength,
  My towering fortress, and my champion,
My God, my rock, where I take refuge,
  My shield, a power to save me, my high stronghold.
Worthy is the Lord to be praised;
  I will call him, and shall be delivered
From all who are against me.

The breakers of death swept round me,
  Torrents of destruction caught up with me,
The cords of darkness, of Sheol, bound me in,
  And death laid a snare before me;
Then in anguish of heart I cried to the Lord,
  I called for help to my God,
And he heard me, even from his lofty temple he heard me.

The earth heaved and quaked,
  Mountains rocked and trembled to the roots
Because he was angry.

Smoke rose from his nostrils,
  Devouring fire came out of his mouth,

Glowing coals issued from him, and flames;
  And as he came down, sweeping aside the heavens
                              while he came,
Thick darkness lay under his feet.
  He rode on the cherubim,
Rode through the air, and swooped with wings of the wind.
  Darkness covered him over at his command,
Dense clouds and black waters out of the skies overcanopied him;
  Ahead of him, out of the brightness there,
Thick cloud swept on, and hail, and cinders red-hot,
  And then in voids of space, the thunder of the Lord,
                              the voice of the Most High!

He loosed his arrows and sped them wide and far;
  He flashed forth lightning shafts, reverberating;
The channelled sea-bed showed itself,
  The foundations of dry land appeared
At thy rebuke, O Lord, and the blasts of thy nostrils' breath.
  He reached from the height of heaven to take me,
He drew me out of many waters;
  From my raging enemy, from those who hated me
And were too strong for me, he rescued me;
  These confronted me in my disastrous day,
But the Lord was there behind me,
  He brought me out into freedom;
He set me at liberty because he delighted in me.
  As I was righteous, so the Lord rewarded me;
As my hands were clean, so he requited me;
  For I kept the ways of the Lord,

24

I did not wickedly cut loose from God,
  I remembered all his laws, I did not deny his decrees.
Thus, having kept myself from my own sinfulness,
  In God's sight I was blameless.
As I was righteous, so the Lord requited me,
  And as he saw my hands were clean.

With the loyal thou showest thyself loyal,
  With the man of integrity thou showest thine own,
With the churlish thou showest thyself churlish;
  Those who are crooked find that thou too art tortuous;
As for humble folk, thou deliverest such,
  But proud looks thou bringest low.

Thou, Lord, dost kindle my lamp,
  Thou, my God, wilt brighten my darkness:
I run at a fence, I leap over a wall, God helping me.
  God's way is perfect, the Lord's word has been tested,
He is a shield to all who take refuge in him.

What god is there but the Lord?
  What rock but our God?
God, who arms me with strength,
  Who makes my way blameless,
Who gives me the feet of a deer
  And sets me secure on the summits,
Who trains my hand to do battle,
  My arms to aim a bronze-tipped arrow.
Thou hast given me thy shield to save me,

With thy right hand thou bearest me up,
Having care for me, thou makest me great.
  Thou givest me room enough for my steps,
My feet have not faltered.
  I chase after enemies, I overtake them
And never turn back until I have broken them;
  I crush them so that they cannot rise any more,
They fall under foot.
  Thou hast armed me with strength to do battle,
Thou subduest my foemen under me,
  Thou hast made them turn their backs before me
And those that hate me I will put to silence.
  Let them cry for help, none will save them now;
Cry even to the Lord: he will not answer.
  I will pound them as fine as wind-blown dust;
I will tread them in like wet mud on the streets.
  Thou wilt deliver me from this medley of struggling people,
Thou wilt make me a master of nations.
  Folk I never knew shall serve me,
As soon as they hear of me they will obey.
  Strange peoples shall cringe to me,
They shall pine away and creep fainting out of their fortresses.

The Lord lives; blessed is my Rock;
  God who saves me is high above all;
God, who grants me full vengeance,
  Who lays nations low beneath me,
Rescues me from the anger of enemies,
  Lifts me high above mine adversaries,

And saves me from men of violence.
  Therefore, O Lord, among the nations I will praise thee,
Singing songs to thy name,
  To One who gives great victories to his king
And in all his doings is loyal to his anointed one,
  To David and his descendants for ever.

ALL heaven above tells out the glories of God,
  Its vault proclaims God's handiwork;
Day pours out speech to day,
  Night reveals knowledge to night,
And this without words or speech,
                    without their voice being heard.

Their music goes out over the wide earth,
  Their tidings to the end of the world.
In them a tent is pitched for the sun,
  Who comes like a bridegroom from under his canopy,
Like an athlete eager and glad to run his race.
  Here, at one end of the sky, the sun arises,
And there at its farthest bound reaches full circuit,
  Nothing can be hidden against its heat.

Perfect is the Lord's law, giving new life to the soul,
  The Lord's word is to be trusted, making the simple wise,
The Lord's teachings are right, they make a heart glad,
  The Lord's command is clear, it is light to the eyes,
Fear of the Lord is unsullied, enduring always,
  The Lord's decrees are true, they are just, one and all,

Better to long for than gold, pure gold in plenty,
  Sweeter than syrup, than honey flowing down from the comb.
By them indeed thy servant is forewarned;
  In keeping them there is great reward;
As for unwitting lapses, who can know them for what they are?
  O, hold me guiltless for faults unknown to me;
Keep back thy servant also from arrogant sinning,
  Let it not master me;
Then I shall be blameless, not guilty of deadly sin.
  May the words that I speak and the thoughts of my heart
Be acceptable to thee, O Lord, my guardian and my rock.

THE LORD give you his answer in the day of distress,
  May the name of Jacob's God set you in a high stronghold.
May he send help from his Sanctuary,
  Lend you support from Zion,
Bear all your gifts in mind,
  Accept the fat of the offerings you burn to him,
Whatever you long for grant you,
  And what you intend bring true;
That we may heartily sing at your victory,
  Exulting in God's name,
The Lord granting you all that you prayed for hitherto!

Now I know that the Lord has granted victory
                                        to his anointed king;
  The Lord will answer him out of his very heaven,
By his right hand, his mighty power to save.
  Others may boast of horses and armaments:
We boast the name of the Lord—our God, the Lord!
  Others waver and sink: we rise and are lifted up in heart.
O Lord, save the king!
  Now, when we call thee, give us our answer, Lord!

O LORD, the king rejoices in thy power;
  He glories greatly in thy deliverance;
Thou hast given him what his heart desired;
  Thou hast not refused him what his lips begged of thee;
Thy rich blessings bid him welcome;
  Thou crownest him with a diadem of pure gold.
Life he asked, and life thou didst give him,
  Life long indeed, enduring for ever and ever.
Through the victory thou hast given him his glory excels;
  Majesty and splendour are bestowed on him by thee;
Thou hast made him worthy of all blessing;
  Thy presence lifts his heart with lively joy.
For the king rests his confidence in the Lord,
  And through the loving care of the Most High
                                    he shall stay unshaken.

With your hand you shall come at all your enemies;
  With your right hand you shall reach to those
                                    that hate you,
So that when you appear they shall be thrust as into
                                    a blazing oven;
  It shall swallow them up, and the fire shall consume them:

It shall destroy their fruits from the earth,
  And their issue from mankind.
For they aimed evil at you,
  Planning a wickedness which they could not perform.
You shall assuredly cause them to turn their backs;
  With taut bowstrings you shall let fly at them.

Be lifted up, O Lord, in thy might!
  We will sing a song of praise to thy strength!

22

MY GOD, my God, why hast thou forsaken me,
   And why art thou far from saving me, far from
                                                my groaning words?
O my God, in the daytime I call thee
   But thou dost not answer;
I call out in the night, and I get no ease;
   Thou art enthroned in holiness,
Thy praises are chanted by Israel.
   In thee our fathers trusted:
They trusted thee, and thou didst deliver them;
   They called to thee, and they were free again;
They trusted thee, and were not brought to shame.

But I am a worm and not a man at all;
   Reproached by men, despised by everyone;
For them, to see me is to mock me,
   To make grimaces at me, nodding their heads my way, saying:
'He committed himself to the Lord for deliverance:
   Let the Lord save him, then, since the man is dear to him!'

Yet thou art the one who drew me forth from the womb,
   Who put me first to my mother's breast.

Upon thee I was cast at birth,
   Thou hast been God to me even from my mother's womb.
Be not far from me, for trouble is near, and no one to help.

Herds of bulls—the mighty beasts of Bashan—surround me
                                    and hem me in,
   They come at me open-mouthed, like roaring and savage lions;
My strength pours away like water; all my bones are out of joint,
   My heart within me melts like wax;
My mouth is dry as a piece of broken pot;
   Tongue cleaves to teeth; I am laid in the dust of death.
Huntsmen come up with me,
   Ill-doers muster about me,
They have hacked off my hands and feet;
   I recount my sufferings over again to them,
While they look on, and gloat,
   Sharing my garments among themselves,
And drawing lots for my cloak.
   But thou, Lord, be thou not far away,
O my help, come quickly to my aid,
   Save me from the sword,
Save, from the power of the dogs, this self that I am,
   Save me from the lion's mouth,
My tortured frame from the horns of buffaloes.

I will declare thy name to all my brothers,
   There in full assembly I will praise thee.
Praise him, you, you who fear the Lord,
   Do him honour, all you sons of Jacob,

Stand, you sons of Israel, in awe of him,
  For he has not despised nor loathed the sufferings of the afflicted,
Nor has he hidden away his face from him;
  But when the afflicted cried to him, he gave him heed.

Through thine own grace do I praise thee in the great assembly;
  I will pay my vows in the sight of those who fear the Lord.
Let the humble eat and be satisfied;
  Let those who seek for the Lord acclaim him;
And may they be glad in heart for ever.
  Let earth to its confines remember and come back to him,
Let all tribes of the nations bend before him;
  For the kingdom is the Lord's; he is ruler of the nations.
How can the buried prostrate themselves,
  Or those who decline into dust bow low before him?
Yet I shall live for him; my children's children shall serve him.
  This shall be told of the Lord to a coming race,
Men shall declare, to a people as yet unborn, his vindication—
  For what he has done.

23

THE LORD is my shepherd: I shall want for nothing.
  He bids me lie down in green pastures;
He leads me along by the side of still waters;
  He renews life within me.
He guides me in paths that are right, for the name
                                              that he bears.

Even though I walk through a valley deep in darkness
  I fear no evil; for thou art with me;
Thy staff and the cudgel in thy hand, these reassure me.

Thou dost set out a table ready before me
  In full sight of my enemies;
And hast lavished oil upon my head;
  My wine-cup is full and brimming over.
Only goodness, and love unfailing, shall follow me
  All the days of my life;
And in the Lord's house shall I make my home
  As long as I live.

THE EARTH is the Lord's and all its fulness,
  The world is his and those who dwell in it;
For he himself founded it on the seas,
  And built it firm on the waters.
Who may ascend the mountain of the Lord?
  Who may stand upright in his holy place?
He whose hands are clean and his heart pure,
  Who has not set his heart on worthless things,
And is not forsworn.
  He shall win blessing from the Lord
And justice from his God, his saviour;
  Such is the destiny of those who look for him,
Who seek the face of the God of Jacob.

Lift up your heads, you gates,
  Lift yourselves up, you everlasting doors,
That the king of glory may come in.
  Who is the king of glory?
The Lord strong and mighty,
  The Lord mighty in battle.
Lift up your heads, you gates,
  Lift them up, you everlasting doors

That the king of glory may come in.
Who then is the king of glory?
The Lord of armies, he is the king of glory.

TO THEE, O Lord, do I lift up my heart.
   I trust in thee my God;
Do not let me be put to shame;
   Do not let enemies triumph over me;
No one who has hope in thee is disappointed;
   But knaves and traitors shall come to shame.
Make thy ways known to me, O Lord;
   Teach me thy paths.
Lead me in thy truth and teach me,
   Thou that savest me, my God: I have waited all
                              day for thee.
Recall thy tender care, O Lord,
   And the constant love of thy dealings long ago.
Do not remember the sins and offences of my youth,
   But think of me, Lord, with thy never-failing love,
And because of thy goodness.
   Good and upright is the Lord;
Therefore he guides sinners in the way,
   Leads humble folk in the path of virtue,
And teaches his way to the meek.
   All the Lord's ways are ways of unfailing love,
Sure for those who abide by his covenant

And his solemn charge.
For the sake of thy name, O Lord, forgive my wickedness,
   Great though it is.
Who, then, is the man that fears the Lord?
   He will learn from the Lord the way he should choose.
He will continue to prosper,
   And his children shall inherit the land.
The secret counsel of the Lord is for those that fear him,
   To them shall he make his covenant known.
My eyes are ever on the Lord
   For he and he alone can free my foot from the snare.
Turn to me and be gracious, for I am alone and in misery.
   Ease my sorrowful heart and bring me out of distress.
Look on my affliction and trouble, and forgive all my sins.
   Watch my enemies, see how many they are,
And how savagely they hate me.
   Protect and deliver me.
Do not let me be shamed, for I take refuge in thee.
   Let integrity and uprightness preserve me,
For my hope, O Lord, is in thee.
   O God, redeem Israel out of all his sorrows.

— 26 —

JUDGE me, Lord: for I have walked in integrity,
   And put unfaltering trust in the Lord.
Examine me, Lord, and test me, thou,
   And prove my most inward heart, and prove my mind.
Thy constant love is ever in my thoughts;
   I walk in thy truth.
I have not spent my time with worthless fellows;
   I do not consort with hypocrites;
I hate the company of evil-doers;
   I will not sit down with the ungodly.
I wash my hands in innocence
   That I may join the procession round thy altar, Lord,
Making thy marvellous doings known,
   Recounting them all with words of gratitude.

O Lord, I love the shelter of thy house,
   Where thy glory dwells;
Gather me not into the company of sinners,
   Nor reckon me among bloodthirsty men
Whose hands purpose evil
   And whose right hands are lavish with bribes.

But I walk in my integrity, O Lord.
  Redeem me and be thou gracious to me;
My feet stand firm on level ground,
  In full assembly will I bless thee, Lord.

— 27 —

THE LORD is my light and my salvation;
   Whom then shall I fear?
The Lord is the refuge of my life;
   Of whom shall I go in dread?
When evil-doers ravenously close in on me
   It is they, my enemies, my haters,
Who stumble and fall;
   An army may encamp before me,
Yet my heart will not fear;
   Fighting may break out against me;
Even so, I shall stay confident.
   Only one thing I ask of the Lord,
And that thing I seek:
   It is that I may make my home, all the days
                                 of my life,
In the Lord's house,
   There to gaze upon the beauty of the Lord
And to seek his will in his temple;
   For he will conceal me in his shelter in my days
                                of trouble,
He will hide me away in the recesses of his tent,
   He will raise me high on a rock.

Now is my head lifted far above my enemies around me.
  With shouts of joy I will sacrifice in his tent,
I will sing songs of praise to the Lord.

Hear, O Lord, when I call aloud,
  Be gracious to me, and answer me.
'Seek his face', my heart has said of thee.
  Thy face, Lord, will I seek.
Do not hide thy face from me,
  Do not angrily turn thy servant away.
Thou hast been my help;
  O do not cast me off, my saviour God,
Do not forsake me.
  Though father and mother should forsake me,
Yet the Lord will have me in his care.
  Show me thy way O Lord; let me not fall into
                              the hands of my greedy foes;
Lead me by a path that is straight to escape my slanderers,
  For they bear lying witness against me
And breathe out violence.
  But I know that I shall look upon the goodness of the Lord
While yet I live;
  Then wait for the Lord, be strong, take courage,
Wait for the Lord.

I CALL out to thee, Lord, I call out;
   Be not deaf to my cry, O my Rock;
Lest if thou ignore me
   I become like those who sink down into the pit.

Hear thou the prayer I utter
   When I cry out to thee,
When I raise my hands towards thy holy shrine.
   Set me not with the ungodly,
These doers of mischief
   Who talk peace with their neighbours
But bear malice in their hearts.
   According to their deeds, their wicked deeds, reward them,
For the work of their hands let them get their deserts;
   They pay no heed to the dealings of the Lord,
Or to the work of his hands;
   Let him tear them down, let him not build them up.

Blessed is the Lord,
   He has heard my supplication,
My strength, my shield, the Lord
   In whom my heart trusts.

And I am helped, my heart exults,
  And with my whole body I give him praise.
The Lord is strength to his people,
  A safe refuge for his anointed king:
O save thy people, bless thine own flock,
  Shepherd them and cherish them for ever.

ASCRIBE to the Lord, you gods,
   Ascribe to him all glory and might;
Ascribe to the Lord the glory due to his name;
   Low before him in holy apparel prostrate yourselves.
The voice of the Lord peals across the waters;
   The God of glory thunders,
The Lord thunders over the unfathomed waters;
   The Lord's voice comes with power,
The Lord's voice with majesty;
   The Lord's voice shatters the cedar trees;
The Lord splinters the cedars of Lebanon,
   The Lord makes Lebanon skip, skip like a calf,
Makes Sirion leap like a young wild ox.
   The voice of the Lord cleaves the lightning-flash.
The voice of the Lord makes the wilderness writhe,
   The Lord makes the wilderness of Kadesh writhe in travail,
The voice of the Lord makes the hinds calve,
   And brings the kids early to birth.
In his temple all cry 'Glory!'
   Over the great flood the Lord sits enthroned,
He has seated himself as king for ever.
   The Lord will give strength to his people,
The Lord will bless his people with peace.

I WILL exalt thy majesty, O Lord;
　For thou hast drawn me from the depths
And hast not let my enemies rejoice over me.

O Lord my God, I cried out to thee,
　And thou didst heal me,
Lord, thou hast brought me up from the shadows,
　Thou hast rescued me alive from among those that
　　　　　　　　　　　　　　go down to the pit.
Sing a psalm to the Lord, all you loyal servants,
　Give thanks to his holy name.
Under his anger men are unquiet; when he is
　　　　　　　　　　　　　gracious they live;
　Weeping comes in the evening to lodge,
But joy enters with the morning;
　And I, while I was free from care, had said:
'I shall never be shaken.'
　In thy favour to me, O Lord,
Thou didst make my mountain fastness secure;
　But when thou didst hide thy face away
I was overcome with horror.
　I called out to thee, O Lord,

I pleaded with thee for grace,
   'What avails my blood' I said, 'if I should go
                               down to the pit?'
'Can dust confess thee? Can it declare thy faithfulness?
   Hear, O Lord, and be gracious to me:
O Lord, be thou my helper!'

Then didst thou turn my tears into dancing,
   Thou didst undo the sackcloth that I wore,
                       and robe me with gladness,
So shall my spirit sing psalms to thee,
   And not be silent,
But for ever confess thee, O Lord my God.

31

IN THEE, Lord, I have found a refuge;
   Let me never be put to shame;
In thy righteousness deliver me;
   Turn thine ear to me, come swiftly to my rescue.
Be thou my rock of refuge,
   A stronghold to keep me safe.
For thou art to me both rock and mighty fortress,
   Lead me, guide me for thine own honour's sake.
Release me from the net they have hidden to snare me;
   Thou art my refuge.
Into thy hands I commit my spirit;
   Thou hast redeemed me, O Lord, thou God of faithfulness.

Thou hatest those who cling to vain deceits;
   But I put my trust in the Lord;
And I will be glad, glad in the constancy of thy love,
   Because thou seest what sorrow I am in,
And in my soul's trouble thou hast cared for me.
   Thou didst not hand me over to the might of the enemy;
Thou hast set my steps free to range over wide country.
   Lord be gracious to me, because I am in trouble;
Grief clouds my eyes,

My life lies waste with sorrow,
And my years with sighing;
  My strength stumbles under its load of misery,
Fever racks my whole frame.
  I have become the reproach of all my enemies,
A burden to my neighbours,
  A horror to those who know me;
All who see me in the street shy away from me,
  I am forgotten like a dead man out of mind,
A thing discarded.
  I hear their mutterings on every side:
                                    'Monster!' they say,
While they conspire together against me,
  Planning to rob me of my life.

But I, Lord, put my trust in thee,
  'Thou art my God', I say,
My fate is in thy hand, O Lord,
  Deliver me from the power of my enemies
                                    and persecutors.
Make thy face shine upon thy servant,
  In thy unfailing love, save me,
Let me not be put to shame, Lord,
  For I have made my appeal to thee.
But shame the wicked,
  Plunge them into the silence of the shadows.
Those lying lips that speak against good men
  So arrogantly and with such proud contempt,
Let them be struck dumb.

How great is thy goodness, Lord,
   Which thou dost keep in store for those who fear thee,
Made manifest before the eyes of men,
   For those who trust in thee.
Thou hidest them by thy presence when men are leagued
                                                against them,
   Thou keepest them safe in shelter from slanderous tongues.
Blessed be the Lord, for he has wrought his miracle of love for me,
   In the time of my distress.
In panic I had cried, 'I am shut out from thy sight!'
   But when I called to thee thou didst hear my plea for grace.

Love the Lord, all you loyal servants;
   The Lord guards the faithful,
But the arrogant he repays in full.
   Be strong, take courage, all you that hope in the Lord.

32

HAPPY he whose disobedience is forgiven,
   Whose sin is covered;
Happy he to whom the Lord imputes no wickedness,
   In whose soul is no deceit!

While I kept silence my whole frame wasted away;
   All day long I lay moaning,
For night and day thy hand was heavy upon me;
   My springs of life turned to summer drought.

Then I acknowledged my sin to thee;
   No longer cloaking my wickedness, I said,
'I will confess my disobedience to the Lord',
   And thou didst forgive the vileness of my sin.
So too, in time of anguish,
   Let every faithful servant offer his prayer to thee;
And then, though swollen waters overflow,
   They shall not come near him.
Be thou my hiding-place; keep danger far away.
   Guard and fold me round with deliverance.

Come, I will instruct you,

And teach you the way you should go, keeping you under my eye.
Do not behave like horse or mule,
 Creatures that lack reason, and must be checked with
               bit and bridle,
Many are the sufferings of the ungodly,
 But the man who trusts in the Lord is surrounded by
             love that never fails.
Be glad, exult in the Lord all righteous men!
 All you whose hearts are true,
Sing loud for joy!

33

SHOUT aloud to the Lord, all you who are righteous;
   Praise well becomes the upright.
Give thanks to the Lord on the lyre,
   Sing him psalms to the ten-stringed lute:
Sing to him a new song,
   Play skilfully, and shout in songs of triumph.
For the Lord's word is right;
   All that he does may be trusted;
Justice he loves, and righteousness;
   The Lord's perpetual love fills the whole earth.

By the word of the Lord the heavens were fashioned;
   He breathed with his spirit, and their starry hosts came forth;
He gathered the ocean's waters as in a water-skin;
   He laid up the deeps in store-chambers.
Let all earth fear the Lord,
   Let the whole earth's company stand in awe before him.
For he spoke, and thus it happened;
   He commanded, and it stood firm.

The Lord brings the plans of nations to nothing;
   He frustrates the counsels of men;

But the plans of the Lord shall stand for ever and ever,
  His purposes are established for generations to come.
Happy that nation which has the Lord for its God;
  Happy are the people he has singled out for his own.
From heaven the Lord looks down;
  From his dwelling-place he espies mankind,
All who live upon earth,
  He who moulds their hearts, every one,
And understands their every deed.

No king is saved by a great army;
  No warrior is delivered by surpassing strength;
In vain does a man trust a horse to save him;
  Strong as it is, it cannot deliver him.
But the Lord's eye rests upon those who fear him,
  Upon those who hope for his never-failing love
To deliver them from death,
  To keep them alive in time of famine.

We have waited eagerly for the Lord,
  He is our help and our shield; and our hearts
                                    are glad in him;
For we have trusted in his holy name.
  O Lord, let thy love be always with us
As we, Lord, hope in thee.

34

AT ALL times I will bless the Lord,
　His praise shall be in my mouth continually.
In the Lord I will boast,
　The humble shall hear me and be glad.
O celebrate the greatness of the Lord with me;
　Let us exalt his name together.
I sought counsel from the Lord, and he answered me,
　He set me free from all my terrors.
Look to him, and let your faces light up;
　Never shall they be abashed.
Here is a poor man who cried out,
　And the Lord heard him;
He rescued him from all his troubles.
　The angel of the Lord encamps about those who fear him,
And delivers them.
　Taste, then, and see how good the Lord is,
Happy the man who turns for refuge to him.

Fear the Lord, you holy ones of his;
　For those who fear him want for nothing.
Unbelievers go poor and hungry,
　But those who seek the Lord want for no good thing.

Come, my sons, listen to me,
  And I will teach you reverence for the Lord.
Who is the man that delights in life?
  Who loves long life that he may enjoy what is good?
Keep your tongue from evil
  And your lips from uttering lies,
Turn away from evil and do good,
  Seek peace, pursue it.
The eyes of the Lord are turned towards the righteous
  And his ears towards their call.
The face of the Lord is set against those that do evil,
  To blot out their very memory from the earth.
When men cry out the Lord hears them
  And sets them free from all their troubles.
The Lord is close by the broken-hearted
  And saves those who are crushed in spirit.
Many are the misfortunes of a good man,
  But from them all the Lord delivers him.
His very bones he guards,
  Not one of them is broken.
Calamity deals death to the wicked,
  And those who hate the righteous are left desolate.
But the Lord ransoms the life of all his servants;
  None are left desolate who trust in him.

40

I WAITED, waited for the Lord:
  He stooped down towards me and heard my crying;
He drew me up out of the slimy pit,
  Out of the mire and clay,
And set my feet upon solid rock.
  And on my lips he put a new song—
'Praise, praise to our God!'

Many a man who sees these things
  Shall turn in reverence to trust the Lord.
For happy is the man who makes the Lord his trust,
  Turning away from liars and braggarts.
Many wonderful things hast thou planned and wrought,
                                        O Lord my God,
  And all for our sake;
With thee no other can compare.
  I would speak of them and tell their story,
                              but they surpass all telling.
If sacrifice and offerings had given thee pleasure,
  Then wouldst thou have made my ear quick to hear thy command.
If thou hadst demanded whole-offering or sin-offering,
  I would have said:

8-2

'Lord, I come! I obey thy will, as the Book requires.'
   In my very soul, O my God, I delight in thy law,
And in the great concourse of the people
                              I have proclaimed thy righteousness.
O Lord thou knowest,
   Thou knowest that I have not sealed my lips.
I have not hidden thy victory in my own heart.
   I have not hidden thy faithfulness and thy saving power,
Nor thy constancy and truth from the great concourse
                                          of the people.
Thou, O Lord, dost not withhold thy tender care from me;
   I am ever sheltered from harm by thy love and thy truth.
But numberless misfortunes hem me in:
   My sins outnumber the very hairs of my head:
My heart dies within me.
   Deign, O Lord, to save me.
O Lord, make haste to my rescue.

Shame them all and bring them to ruin,
   Those men who seek my downfall!
They are delighted by my misery—oh,
                        hurl them backwards and humiliate them!
   Make them stagger under the weight of their ignominy,
Who fling scorn upon me.
   But to those who seek thee
Give the joy and the gladness of thy presence;
   And let all who love thy saving power,
Cry 'The Lord is great.'

But as for me, O Lord, I am poor.
   I am in great need—O Lord, think of me.
Thou only canst help and save me.
   Delay not long, my God.

41

HE who takes thought for the helpless, happy is he;
   In the day of trouble the Lord delivers him.
The Lord protects him and so saves him alive,
   Making him a power in the land,
Nor leaves him to be devoured by the greed of his enemies.

When he lies sick the Lord nurses him,
   Turning his mattress for him, when he is ill.
So, for my part, I said,
   'Be gracious, O Lord; heal me, though I have
                              sinned against thee';
My enemies think I am at death's door.
   'How soon will he die', they ask, 'and
                              his name perish?'
If any comes to see me his words are hollow,
   In malice he looks for the worst,
Then goes out and spreads his tale.
   They who hate me whisper together,
Forecasting my speedy end.
   'His sickness is fatal', they say,
'He will never leave the bed on which he lies.'
   Even the friend whom I trusted,

62

Who ate at my own table,
  Has stabbed me in the back.

But, Lord, be gracious to me, Lord, restore me,
  So that I may fully repay them.
By this I shall know that thou dost delight in me,
  And that my enemy will never triumph over me:
Thou dost support me because of my innocence,
  Thou dost set me up before thee, Lord, for evermore.

Blessed be the Lord, the God of Israel,
  From everlasting to everlasting.
Amen and Amen.

For EU product safety concerns, contact us at Calle de José Abascal, 56–1°,
28003 Madrid, Spain or eugpsr@cambridge.org.

www.ingramcontent.com/pod-product-compliance
Ingram Content Group UK Ltd.
Pitfield, Milton Keynes, MK11 3LW, UK
UKHW030902150625
459647UK00021B/2655